DANGER ON THE MOUNTAIN!

True Stories of Extreme Adventures!

Gregg Treinish
With Kitson Jazynka

NATIONAL GEOGRAPHIC

WASHINGTON, D.C.

Since 1888, the National Geographic
Society has funded more than 12,000
research, exploration, and preservation
projects around the world. The Society
receives funds from National Geographic
Partners LLC, funded in part by your
purchase. A portion of the proceeds from this
book supports this vital work. To learn more,
visit www.natgeo.com/info.

For more information, visit
www.nationalgeographic.com, call
1-800-647-5463, or write to the
following address:

National Geographic Partners
1145 17th Street N.W.
Washington, D.C. 20036-4688 U.S.A.

Visit us online at nationalgeographic.com/books

For librarians and teachers:
ngchildrensbooks.org

More for kids from National Geographic:
kids.nationalgeographic.com

For information about special discounts for
bulk purchases, please contact National
Geographic Books Special Sales:
ngspecsales@ngs.org

For rights or permissions inquiries, please
contact National Geographic Books Subsidiary
Rights: ngbookrights@ngs.org

Art directed by Sanjida Rashid
Designed by Ruth Ann Thompson

National Geographic supports K–12
educators with ELA Common Core
Resources. Visit natgeoed.org/
commoncore for more information.

Trade paperback
ISBN: 978-1-4263-2565-6
Reinforced library edition
ISBN: 978-1-4263-2566-3

Printed in China
16/RRDS/1

Table of CONTENTS

ENDLESS ADVENTURE

Explorer Gregg Treinish enjoys the view from the top of a mountain.

Skittish horses kick up dirt in their corral.

Chapter 1

OUT OF CONTROL

The pounding of horses' hooves was like thunder in my ears. I knew I was in trouble when the frothy white foam from my horse's mouth flew back and hit me in the face. I clung to his sweaty neck as he sprinted. I felt completely out of control.

This had all been my dad's idea. My family was on a six-week, cross-country trip out West. My dad had been talking about doing this trip my whole life. When we left the Ohio, U.S.A., suburbs, I had no idea what was ahead, but I couldn't wait. I loved the idea of journeying into the unknown.

So far, the trip had been amazing. We had searched for grizzly bears in Yellowstone National Park. We had raced go-karts in Wisconsin, visited Mount Rushmore in South Dakota, and hiked in the Grand Canyon in Arizona. Now we were in Nevada.

On this day, my dad wanted to take my brothers and me horseback riding in the foothills of the gigantic, snow-capped Sierra Nevada mountains.

I followed my brothers out of the RV and headed toward a dusty, run-down barn. But my excitement turned into something else as soon as I saw the horses.

Right away, I could tell that the horses weren't well cared for. They were dirty and skittish. They tossed their heads as if they were afraid.

The man getting the horses ready dropped heavy western saddles on their backs. The horses sidestepped and snorted. He yelled at them to stand still while he tightened the saddles to keep them from slipping. We mounted up. But the horses wouldn't move.

The man smacked them to make them walk out of the corral. I had a sick feeling in my stomach for the animals.

But once we left the corral, I started to feel something else. I loved the powerful feeling of riding a horse. My body fell into a rhythm with the horse's motion as he walked forward. I gripped the cracked leather reins that rested across his neck, and I looked out toward the mountains. I took a deep breath and closed my eyes for a moment.

As soon as we got away from the barn, my horse threw his head up and walked faster through the lush prairie. The other horses walked a little faster, too.

I wondered if the horses had planned an escape.

Then my horse leaped forward. I lurched back. Now we

were trotting, *one-two, one-two, one-two,* faster and faster. I bounced hard with each quick step and yelled for him to stop.

But the horse didn't stop. He lowered his head and charged across the meadow like a runaway train. I held my breath and struggled to balance as the horse plunged forward. We skimmed over rocks and wove around bushes and logs. I dug my fingers into his tangled mane as I clung to his neck.

The other horses raced, too. My dad held on to my little brother David's shirt as he dangled off the side of the horse they shared. David screamed and cried.

Eventually, the horses got tired. Somehow, we got back to the barn without falling off or killing ourselves.

My brothers and my dad got off and said they never wanted to ride horses again. But I loved the rush of tearing across that open range. I also really, really wished I could have helped those horses. I could feel their misery. This crazy ride left a strong impression on me as a kid.

Today, I'm a biologist (sounds like bye-OL-uh-jist). Ever since I was a kid, I have loved outdoor adventure. And I've always wanted to make a positive impact on the world.

I founded an organization called Adventure Scientists. We match extreme outdoor athletes (like hikers, paddlers, and skiers) with information-hungry scientists who need data samples from hard-to-reach places all over the world.

Think Like a Biologist

I once hiked for 520 miles
(837 km) in the Northern
Rocky Mountains to study wild
animals like wolverines, moose,
mountain lions, and grizzly bears.
I collected information to help protect
those species and their wild homes, but
I also became part of the ecosystem
(sounds like EE-koh-sis-tum) myself.
If you see a wild animal, you can think like
a biologist, too. Imagine yourself as the
animal. View the world from the animal's
eyes. Ask yourself questions about how
the animal might act or how it finds food.

Even though I grew up in the suburbs, I saw beauty in nature and animals all around me. I had a few wild "pets" at home, like the chipmunk that lived under our garage. I called him Chippy.

I loved Chippy. I'd sit and wait for him to show up. Then I'd watch him run around. There was a stray cat I used to watch for, too. I called him Mr. Whiskers.

Looking back, I realize it was my connection with animals that started me on the path to become a biologist, and to start Adventure Scientists. As a kid, I thought a lot about how animals survived despite the challenges of their environments.

I had struggles in my own environment, too. I got in trouble a lot. That summer of our trip out West, I spent a lot of time in the bathroom of the RV. That's where my parents made me sit if I was harassing my brothers too much.

I saw a lot of Yellowstone National Park through the bathroom window, including animals like bison, elk, and eagles. I really wanted to see a grizzly bear on that trip, but we never did.

When I got back home and started the eighth grade, life was hard then, too. I made fun of other kids. As a result, I didn't have many friends. I was usually the kid people's parents didn't want their kid to be friends with. That made school tough.

But outdoors, things were different. I always felt more comfortable outdoors than indoors. So I became an explorer.

The pristine wilderness awaited Gregg in Garibaldi Park, north of Vancouver.

Chapter 2

PUSHING BOUNDARIES

I could hardly hear anything except my own heavy breathing as I struggled up the steep ridge trail. My pulse throbbed in my ears. To make it to the top, I focused on a single tree up ahead. Ten more steps to reach it. Then I'd pick another towering pine tree and make a goal to reach that.

I was 16 now. Dealing with other kids at school had gotten harder for me. I tried to stay out of trouble, but it never seemed to work. I didn't want to follow the rules. I pushed boundaries with my parents and my teachers.

My grandma Mandu seemed to sense that an outdoor adventure might help me. She offered to send me on a guided, three-week summer wilderness trek on the coast of British Columbia, Canada. I couldn't wait to go. But once I was there, I was having a tough time. It was hard.

The rocky trail stretched out long and steep in front of us. We were in Garibaldi Park, a pristine wilderness north of Vancouver, Canada. I tried not to think about the weight of the pack on my back. Hardly anyone talked as our group slowly trudged up the hill.

The kid in front of me was slow. He
kept stumbling and crying and holding
up the group. We could only go as fast as
our slowest member. I was getting upset
with him.

Then he fell. Our
guide, Guybe (sounds
like GUY-bee) was quick
to help. Guybe asked us
to divide up the stuff in
the kid's pack and help
him carry it. It had never occurred to me
to offer to help. But I realized that was the
quickest way to get to the top. I knew
I was strong enough to carry a little more.

Guybe unzipped the kid's pack.
I reached in and grabbed a five-pound
(2.3-kg) bag of apples and put it in

Did You Know?

Garibaldi Park is
home to mountain
goats, grizzly bears,
bald eagles,
and endangered
trumpeter swans.

my own pack. I carried it the rest of the day. Helping was a new thing for me. I was part of a team. I was doing something right. For once, I was not in trouble. That was a big deal.

I admired Guybe. He seemed fearless. He also had a lot of wilderness experience. Guybe had been a thru-hiker on the Appalachian (sounds like ap-uh-LAY-chun) Trail. That means he had walked the whole 2,190 miles (3,524 km) from Georgia to Maine, U.S.A.

Guybe and I talked a lot about long hikes. He told me he thought I could do a hike like the Appalachian Trail. I wasn't so sure. Maybe I could do the Buckeye Trail. That's the long-distance trail that loops around my home state of Ohio.

That might be something I could do. But I wasn't so sure I could do anything quite like Guybe did. To me, he was a mythical creature.

Once during that three-week summer trek, he helped our whole group get through a scary situation. The trail had washed out after a storm. Thinking there was no way to get across, we stopped short. To our left was a wall of dirt and rocks that spilled across where the trail had been. To the right, the earth dropped off. I didn't see how we could get around it.

Guybe skipped across the loose, wet rocks in his sandals. Then he looked back and told us "c'mon," like it was nothing.

Land Snorkeling

A friend of mine refers to hiking as "land snorkeling." You can see a lot when you're on foot. When you walk through the woods—as opposed to driving or being on a bike—you notice everything. You see animals moving through the shadows. You see the bark on the trees. I always tell people to "hike their own hike." Go where you want to go. Stop when you want to stop. And take your time as you land snorkel through the woods.

A couple of kids made it across the 10-foot (3-m) gash in the trail. But when it was my turn, I looked over the edge to the right. Roots dangled out from the side of the hill. Sharp rocks were piled a long way down below. My heart pounded. My feet wouldn't move.

Guybe looked at me. "You can do it," he said, "just go fast."

I took a deep breath and launched. I went fast. The rocks skittered under my feet. I slipped and stumbled and went down on one knee. I heard the smash of a rock as it sailed over the edge and landed against another rock down below. I couldn't believe I wasn't dead yet.

Guybe had a way of making me believe in myself. I focused on his calm voice.

I got up. I kept going. It all happened kind of fast. Suddenly, I was on the other side. I was terrified! But I was also laughing and talking with the other kids about the crossing. It was like pushing a boundary in a different kind of way. I had pushed myself.

Another time on that trip, we paddled sea kayaks around an unpopulated island off the coast of Vancouver. When a summer storm rolled in, I felt like I was paddling through a cloud. There was so much rain and mist that I couldn't see a thing. I was cold and wet and had no idea where I was going.

Did You Know?

Early Arctic nomads hunted in hand-carved sea kayaks.

But I had trust in my guide, and I was gaining trust in myself.

After our group paddled to shore, climbed out onto the beach, and secured our stuff, Guybe taught us how to build a sauna on the beach. It was a fun way to get warm. We dragged branches and logs in from the woods. We set them up and built a teepee with a tarp. Then we built a fire inside it and put rocks on the fire. When the rocks got hot, we poured salt water on them. Warm steam filled our makeshift teepee. I breathed in the warm, salty air, feeling tired but strong and resourceful.

A herder riding a Siberian reindeer passes Gregg one day on the expedition.

Chapter 3

WILD FOR WOLVERINES

There are a lot of things on my to-do list, but getting licked on the face by a reindeer has never been one of them. Tell that to the reindeer! I was 31 years old and on a skiing expedition (sounds like eks-puh-DISH-un) in the northernmost part of Mongolia (sounds like mon-GOLE-ee-ya). We had paused for a moment to take in the scene.

We were surprised to see reindeer. There were about two dozen of them standing in the snowy field. They crowded around us to have a better look. That's when one must have thought that a closer look wasn't enough. A taste might be better. It was like being licked by a 200-pound (90-kg) puppy. Wow! I hadn't signed up for this!

Well, maybe I had. I was leading this expedition in Mongolia's remote Darhad Valley. We hadn't been looking for reindeer, though. Our goal was to learn more about wolverines (sounds like WUL-vuh-reens).

Wolverines are the largest animals in the weasel family. A wolverine is stocky and muscular, like a small bear. It's a solitary (sounds like SAH-li-ter-ee) animal, too. That means it likes to keep to itself. And that's one reason we were skiing through this cold landscape. A wolverine can be hard to find.

One day during our search, we came across nomadic (sounds like noh-MAD-ik) herders. They were migrating. They had trekked down a mountain in a parade of Mongolian horses. With them were thousands of camels, oxen, sheep, yaks, and goats. There were people riding horseback carrying calves in their laps. I remember seeing a big ox pulling a calf on a sled. I'd never seen animals carrying animals before. For two full days, we skied up into the mountains while they walked down. Sometimes we stopped long enough to enjoy a meal with them. We ate dinner in a ger (sounds like GARE). That's a portable, round tent covered with animal hide. These people taught us a lot about this wild, extreme place.

One morning, I crunched through the ice, snapped on my skis, and slid out onto the ice-covered snow. The sun had melted some of the snow the day before. But it had refrozen overnight. Now there was a thick, slick surface that was easy to ski on. With a windchill below zero (−17.8°C), I was pretty cold. Soon my goggles would be crusted over and icicles would be dripping from my nose. Yet I was grateful for this cold. It would keep the layer of ice on the snow.

If the weather warmed up even a little, the ice would start to melt again. And even a little melting would mean trouble for us. It would make the snow too mushy.

Wolverines in the Wild

Wolverines in northern Mongolia survive some of the coldest, harshest winter conditions on Earth. Yet trapping and habitat loss pose a major threat to the species. Climate change likely threatens wolverines as well. This species is a clear example of how humans can change an ecosystem for the worse. The data we collected on this trip will help Mongolian conservationists study the species and learn more about this incredible, cold habitat.

This had happened before, and we had to trudge for hours up to our waists in what felt like mashed potatoes!

Traveling on top of the ice wearing cross-country skis meant we could move quickly and easily. Skiing also made us feel like were part of this frozen ecosystem.

We hadn't seen any wolverines on our expedition yet, but one way to track an animal is to follow where it's been. Over weeks of searching, we picked up 27 sets of tracks. We found something else, too. It's called "scat." That's basically wild-animal poop. You won't believe me, but I was thrilled that we found 33 samples of scat! Maybe it sounds gross. But it told us that wolverines were nearby, and it allowed us to collect genetic material from them.

We found fur
samples, too.
Each sample was
important. Until our
expedition, no western
researchers had ever
collected DNA samples
from a live wolverine in this region. The
data we collected could give researchers
clues about the wolverine population.

I was dying to see a wolverine up close.
We never did. We spent nearly a month
searching. We skied 230 miles (370 km)
through the high mountains. We skied
across frozen rivers and trudged through
the collapsing snow. I didn't see one
wolverine. But I saw the power of what an
adventurer can accomplish.

Gregg warms himself in the sun one morning during his long hike along the Appalachian Trail.

THREE
SECONDS
OF COURAGE

Staying in the raft is one major goal on the Arkansas River in Colorado, U.S.A.!

ONE FOOT
IN FRONT OF
THE OTHER

The deep, frosty water of the Arkansas (sounds like AR-kan-saw) River churns white as it rushes over the rapids called Frog Rock. The spot can be found in the shadows of the Colorado Rocky Mountains. It's framed by huge rocks, evergreens, and—on that spring day— a low ceiling of ominous clouds.

I was trying out for a summer job as a white-water rafting guide.

I had never steered a raft before, though!

Well, this would be like some of my other adventures, I told myself. I grabbed my paddle and jumped in the raft. The rushing water, mostly snowmelt from the Rockies, was cold, cold, cold.

A mile (1.6 km) or so down the river, the water curled and sprayed in huge arcs against a tumble of boulders. I misjudged the rapid. The raft hit a rock and bounced hard to the left. I flew out of the boat into the unfriendly water.

The heavy raft, still carrying my passengers, surged over me. The weight of the boat held me under in darkness. I couldn't breathe. I choked back river water. The water pulsed past me. I couldn't get to the surface.

I felt my way to the edge of the boat, trying not to panic. After what seemed like an eternity, I popped up into the air and took a ragged breath. The others reached for me. I grabbed their hands and climbed back onto the raft.

The instructor asked if I was still good to go. I coughed, wiped my face, and said, "I got this." We finished the run.

I left that day not knowing if I had the job, but that event helped me believe I could do great work in the outdoors. I had been reading a book called *A Walk in the Woods* by Bill Bryson. It's a fantastic memoir (sounds like MEM-wahr) about a man who hiked a section of the Appalachian Trail.

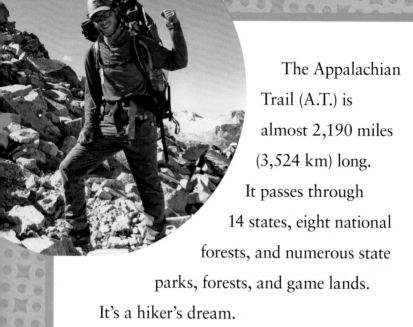

The Appalachian Trail (A.T.) is almost 2,190 miles (3,524 km) long. It passes through 14 states, eight national forests, and numerous state parks, forests, and game lands. It's a hiker's dream.

Something about that book grabbed my attention. I couldn't stop reading. When I read the last page, I knew what I wanted to do. I walked into the living room and told my roommate I was going to hike the A.T. the next spring. That's the best time to start so you finish before winter. Plus, I had a lot of preparation and planning to get through first.

As luck would have it, I got the job as a white-water rafting guide. That summer, I worked on the river three days a week. I also worked as a preschool teacher to make extra money. And I prepared for the Appalachian Trail.

I planned every detail of the hike down to the tenth of a mile. I read books about the trail and built my strength on training hikes with my backpack full of bricks and firewood. While the preschool kids napped, I plotted out where I'd resupply and exactly how far I'd walk each day.

I think the planning was a way to trick myself into believing I was ready. In reality, I was pretty inexperienced. While the A.T. is an established trail, there's no telling what your experience will be or even if you'll finish.

All the while I was preparing, my mom was worrying. She didn't like the idea of me hiking alone. She thought I'd be killed by a black bear. But I was set on going. I told her black bears rarely attack people.

Did You Know?

Black bears live in the eastern United States. They are smaller and less aggressive than grizzly bears.

In March, my parents met me in Georgia and drove me to the trailhead. Together, we hiked up Springer Mountain to the southern start. My parents were excited for me. We had a tearful goodbye.

Fifteen minutes later, I ended up back at the parking lot. It turns out, the trail north crosses south before it heads north again. I was confused and frustrated.

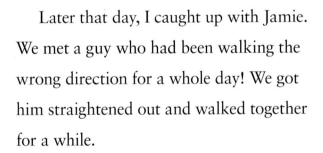

I met another hiker also walking the wrong way. His name was Jamie. Together, we figured out where to begin. Jamie set off ahead. I hugged my parents again and walked off alone. I was scared and excited at the same time.

Later that day, I caught up with Jamie. We met a guy who had been walking the wrong direction for a whole day! We got him straightened out and walked together for a while.

In those first couple of days, my pack weighed 45 pounds (20.4 kg). That's pretty heavy—about as much as carrying 6 gallons (23 L) of water on my back.

Trail Names

Just about everybody thru-hiking the Appalachian Trail gets a trail name. It's usually suggested by another thru-hiker. Near the start of my hike, a hiker named me "Ski Bum." She said I never stopped talking about skiing. I liked it. Halfway through the trail, my name was shortened to "Bum." Some of my friends on the trail were Rooster, Gordy, Big Stick, Coyote, Little Munchkin, Lumber, and Lord Duke.

On day three, I met an experienced thru-hiker. His trail name was Tucson (sounds like TOO-sawn). He said my pack was way too heavy. He offered to help lighten it up. He told me that I could live without soap, bug spray, sunscreen, trail maps, and extra pants. He tossed my water shoes out and taught me how to make flip-flops with the liners of my hiking shoes. I thought he was a little crazy, but he had a lot of experience and gave me good advice.

Among other things, I kept my tent, sleeping bag, rain jacket, a toothbrush, toothpaste, a journal, a spoon, a small stove, and a pen. My backpack lightened up to 19 pounds (8.6 kg). I felt pretty good about the choices I'd made. After that, it was just one foot in front of the other.

Fog is often present in the mornings along the Appalachian Trail.

Chapter 2

PAINFUL LESSONS

A gentle spring rain fell as I walked through a field in Virginia's Grayson Highlands. I'd been on the A.T. for about two months now. I saw a group of wild ponies huddled near the tree line. I wondered if they knew something I didn't. I looked over my shoulder. Dark clouds were looming. I zipped up my jacket and picked up the pace. A major storm was on its way, and the skies were about to open.

A streak of lightning lit up the dark clouds. At the same time, thunder cracked so loud that the puddles in the grass rippled from the force of it. The rain came down heavier. I ran toward the edge of the forest and was soaked by the time I reached it. The storm was really violent. And it was about to get a lot worse.

Growing up in Ohio, I'd seen hail before, but nothing quite like what fell from the sky next. Like ice missiles, huge clumps of hail rained down.

There was little to offer me protection. The hail struck me and nicked at my ears. Blood dripped down my neck. I pulled my pack off my back and held it over my head.

Then I ran, looking for some kind of cover while I tried to keep moving.

At one point, I ran past a family. They had been out for a hike but were now taking shelter under a big rock outcropping. They yelled to me, asking if I had any idea how long the storm would last. I didn't, of course. But I yelled back, "I hope it never ends!"

The truth was, being caught in the middle of this storm made me feel like a wild animal. I loved it. This is what extreme adventure felt like! This is what it felt like to be on my own.

The rain eventually died down some, and the hail stopped falling. But I probably

Did You Know?

Hail is precipitation that falls in icy chunks, or "hailstones." They can be as small as a grain of rice or as big as a baseball.

hiked another 15 miles (24 km) in rain that day. At dusk, I pulled on my headlamp, left the trail, and walked through the woods. I looked for a lean-to, one of the many three-sided wooden shelters found along the trail. I ate granola bars for dinner that night and slept inside the shelter in my sleeping bag. The day had been so exciting, I slept really well.

Did You Know?

The Appalachian Trail in northern Pennsylvania is known for its rocky ridges and steep hills.

About a month later, I reached Pennsylvania. I had covered about 300 miles (483 km) at a pace of up to 40 miles (64 km) a day. That's a pretty standard pace for a thru-hiker. I was more than halfway through the hike, walking north with the onset of spring.

Here's something you should know about me and walking: I am not the most graceful person. My friends have always described my way of walking as "controlled falling." And during all these months, I had fallen many times. My hands were scraped and bruised. I had ripped my only pair of pants over and over. It was not pretty.

The trail changes in Pennsylvania. It narrows. Jagged rocks riddle the path. The more I walked—and the more I fell—the more I began to wonder what the point of this six-month walk was.

On one memorable day, I was seriously "bonking," or running out of energy. I had hiked a little more than 15 miles (24 km), but I was struggling.

Part of the problem was that I couldn't carry—or eat—enough food to keep up with the calories I burned walking up and down hills all day. An average thru-hiker burns between 7,000 and 10,000 calories a day, which is the equivalent of nearly 20 hamburgers. Or close to 75 granola bars. That's a lot of food.

That day, I was tired, cold, and dehydrated. It had been raining for days. The trail was shadowy and slick. I was soaked from head to toe. My shoes were falling apart. That's when I tripped for what seemed like the 14th time that day.

I twisted and scraped my ankle and was bleeding, again. It seemed like I was always scraped and bleeding. I sat down in the drizzle. I was overcome with exhaustion, frustration, and doubt. I grabbed a big rock. I held it in my hand and felt the weight of it. Then I chucked it at a tree. The rock gouged the tree's soft bark. As soon as I threw it, I regretted it. I hadn't meant to damage the tree. Suddenly, I felt like the most selfish person in the world. What was I doing out here hurting trees? I sat there and cried as the rain soaked me even more.

After a while, it hit me: I needed to stay positive. I needed to focus on my goal. I vowed to get to the end of the trail. But there was something else, too. Hurting that tree reminded me that I wanted to make a positive difference in the world. I made a promise to myself that I'd make my time outdoors count for something.

I thought about my dad and a quote he brought home from work one day when I was a kid. He taped it to the fridge so my brothers and I could see it. It said, "Attitude is everything." I realized I had the ability to change my attitude in any situation. I could make it better.

My ankle was still bleeding. I was still tired and hungry. I got up and walked on.

Trail Magic

Trail "angels" dedicate time, money, and energy to helping people along the Appalachian Trail. They leave behind "magic," like cans of soda chilling in a stream or a cooler filled with barbecued chicken for hikers. One time my friend Rooster and I hiked 44 miles (71 km) in a single day. We stayed in a hiker hostel that night. The next morning, a woman people call Trail Angel Mary fed us an incredible feast. There's a general idea among hikers on the A.T. that everything will work out. People like Trail Angel Mary are a big part of that.

Coming face-to-face with a moose is not something an explorer forgets.

Chapter 3

MOOSE ON THE LOOSE

It was the sound of heaving that woke me up. Like a dog throwing up. I was "cowboy camping" in Maine. With no tent, it was just me, my sleeping bag, and the stars. Or so I thought. I thought the sound was Kaya, my friend Little Munchkin's dog. They were camped nearby. I yelled at Kaya to go away. But it wasn't Kaya. I opened my eyes. A giant

Did You Know?

Moose feed on aquatic plants and are great swimmers, sometimes paddling several miles at a time.

pair of fuzzy nostrils quivered in my face. A huge male moose was looking down at me. A warm mist blasted my face when he exhaled. I yelped. He grunted and reared up. Then he slammed his front hooves down, one on either side of my face. I froze.

Seconds later, he leaped over me and took off running. The massive animal then crashed through the rope holding the hammock where my friend Gordy slept. She dropped to the ground, yelling. She had been in a dead sleep and thought it was me, joking around. Rooster ran out of his tent like a crazy person yelling, "Big moose! Big moose!"

The moose stood about seven feet (2 m) high at the shoulders and had antlers as wide as I am tall. He continued running toward the woods. Then he stopped and looked back. I was afraid he was coming back to trample us or gore us with his antlers. But he just looked at us like he was confused. Then he turned around and waded into the nearby lake.

In the lake, we saw a cow (that's what you call a female moose) and a calf waiting for him. They swam across the lake together like nothing had happened. As for me, I still cowboy camp. But I keep my sleeping bag closer to other campers now.

They don't call this mossy, rain-soaked part of the trail in Maine the "100 Mile Wilderness" for nothing. This last stretch runs over remote mountains and beautiful lakes in Maine's Baxter State Park. It's gorgeous, but rocky, isolated, and tough to get through.

At this point, I had walked about 2,000 miles (3,219 km). I felt proud, like I was on the verge of accomplishing something great.

Looking out over a cold mountain pass on the trail, I saw the fall leaves bursting with color. The sight of it almost overwhelmed me.

Ever since that awful moment when I damaged the tree in Pennsylvania, I had been thinking about my life and what should come next for me. With fewer than 200 miles (320 km) to go before the trail's end, I trekked off trail to find a pay phone.

I made calls to a few companies where I might be able to get a job working in wilderness therapy for kids. It seemed like a good way for me to start giving back.

After walking for a total of six months and eight days on the trail, I finally reached the end. On my last day, I summited Mt. Katahdin with about 25 of my trail friends. It was one of the most beautiful days of my life. To this day, October 8 is like a national holiday to me.

Through all those miles walked, I figured something out: It only takes three seconds of courage to follow your dream. One second to assess and pick your head

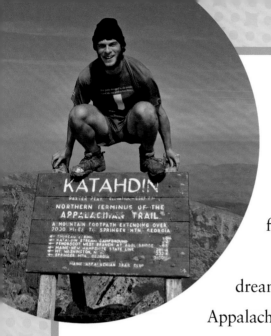

up; one second to see where you're going; and one second to take the first step.

At first my dream was to hike the Appalachian Trail. Then my dream became putting my time outdoors to good use. Becoming a wilderness therapy instructor was a first step for me. It was the first time I'd actually be taking what I knew about the outdoors and truly helping others.

For the next two years, I followed that dream. I worked as a wilderness therapy instructor. Facing and overcoming the challenges that the wilderness presents—whether it's a washed-out trail, a rock slide, or going hungry—is incredibly powerful.

You look back and see that you made it through, despite the challenges. It's a powerful way to learn that there's little you can't accomplish if you stick with it and use your creativity and resources to solve problems.

Time outdoors is also healing. I really connected with the kids I worked with in wilderness therapy. I loved giving them the chance to make it up tough peaks and then look back on what they had achieved. I hiked those peaks with them. It was not easy stuff. But I loved watching them feel that pride of making it through. I felt it, too.

Save a Moose

Moose are built for mobility. Long legs and tough hooves help a moose climb over logs and trek through deep snow. But this sensational species can't outrun ticks. Helped by our warming environment, invasions of these blood-sucking, disease-carrying arachnids have caused moose populations to decline. You can help moose outrun this

devastating problem.
Talk to your parents
about driving less
and using less heat
and air-conditioning.
Lowering your
family's energy use
helps slow climate change.
That might just help a moose.

DANGER
ON THE
MOUNTAIN!

Gregg takes in the spectacular view in the Andes Mountains.

A blanket of clouds gathers at Gregg's feet in the Andes Mountains.

WALKING ON CLOUDS

Thorns tore my pants and scratched my face and arms. I kept walking. My backpack strap broke. I kept walking. It was the first day of a two-year trek across the Andes (sounds like ANN-deez) Mountains. Nothing was going well. My hiking partner had already slipped in a creek and fractured her wrist. Now we had taken a wrong turn.

We stood on the mountain wondering if this expedition had been a mistake.

The Andes Mountains are located in South America, running north to south along the western coast of the continent. These mountains are the longest and one of the highest mountain ranges in the world.

My hiking partner and friend, Deia (sounds like DAY-uh), and I stood on a spot just south of the Equator. Our goal was to explore the Andes, learning about the mountains and the region's culture. We also wanted to learn about sustainability and spread the message of conserving resources.

We would travel along llama paths, train tracks, and ancient foot trails across this massive mountain range. We'd planned to document our adventures by blogging, photographing, and recording videos to share what we learned.

We had spent a great deal of time preparing for this expedition, but you would not have known it to see us.

Despite our attempts, we couldn't find a map of the area before we left. So it was easy for us to take a wrong turn. We were hoping to reach a certain mountain lake by the afternoon. Yet after wandering for hours, we finally set up camp in the dark near some thermal springs.

Without freshwater from the lake, we didn't have water to cook with. Dinner

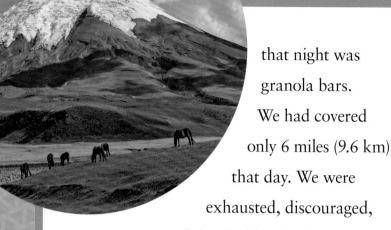

that night was granola bars. We had covered only 6 miles (9.6 km) that day. We were exhausted, discouraged, and shocked by the physical difficulties we had already encountered.

The next morning, we woke up with the sun. We packed up camp, checked our compass, and set out. We hiked all day and finally reached the lake by dinnertime. Dinner was noodles and broth, which we ate as a herd of wild horses passed by.

For days, we walked and climbed and walked and climbed. At last, we crossed a ridge. On the other side, I saw what I'd been waiting to see for a year:

Cotopaxi (sounds like co-toh-PAX-see). Cotopaxi is a massive volcano. Its name is sometimes translated as "neck of the moon." We called it "the Pax." It spans nearly 14 miles (22 km) across and rises 19,800 feet (6,035 m) into the sky.

With almost 90 known eruptions, Cotopaxi is one of Ecuador's most active volcanoes. Deia and I were overwhelmed by its beauty. Being this high up in altitude made me feel like we were walking on clouds.

The Pax was the first of many incredible things we would see on this adventure. Every day, the Andes amazed us with dazzling sunrises,

> **Did You Know?**
>
> **In 2015, Cotopaxi showed signs of increased activity. Hundreds of small earthquakes were recorded.**

wildlife, and misty sunsets. The rich colors of everything we saw—greens, browns, reds, and purples—were greater than the greatest painter could imagine.

To hike the Andes means a lot of ups and downs. The Andes has a vast range of elevations (sounds like el-uh-VAY-shuhns). When you change elevation, the climate often changes, too.

You can start the day in a tropical jungle, then pass through a pine forest, and farther along, you can step into a desert. Some mornings, we woke up with frozen water bottles, but by afternoon, we were sweating in 95°F (35°C) heat! We always had to adjust.

After about eight months, we had hiked more than 2,000 miles (3,219 km).

Yet we hadn't reached our halfway point. We still had about 5,500 miles (8,800 km) to go. Things had been going smoothly for a while, but I knew I was in trouble now.

We had just resupplied in a small town in southern Ecuador. About 5 miles (8 km) down a dirt road outside of town, I had to stop.

We had already endured (sounds like en-DURD) a lot on this trip. I'd shivered through high fevers. I'd suffered through stomach bugs. Once, we went without water for three days. But now, there was a pain in my heel that was so serious, I had to stop walking. It was time to get help.

A passing truck gave us a ride to a nearby hospital. It was a Sunday. The hospital was closed. We found a phone and called the number left on a note on the hospital door. After a long wait, the doctor arrived.

He held my foot in his hands to examine it. When he pushed on the sore spot with his finger, I yelled. The pain was terrible. The doctor studied my heel. Then he shook his head and said, "This is not good."

He pressed harder. I winced and gritted my teeth. The sore spot erupted. Thousands of tiny white things—smaller than grains of rice—poured out. They were worm eggs.

The doctor used a sharp knife to scrape

more of the tiny worm eggs out of my heel. Then he used tweezers to pull out a squirming red worm from the middle of it all. It was the mother.

The doctor said the eggs had been there for a while. And that they might have been only hours away from hatching into little worms, like the mother. If that had happened, the worms wouldn't have stayed in my heel. They could have traveled up to my lungs and killed me.

The doctor cleaned my heel and bandaged it to keep it dry. My foot still hurt but not as bad as before. Even with some pain, I knew I was lucky. We got back on the road again and headed to the trail. Soon we'd say goodbye to Ecuador and head south into Peru (sounds like puh-ROO).

Swimming with Piranhas

Part of our travels through Peru took us into the Amazon rain forest. Here, everything felt alive. Birds peep, screech, whistle, and caw. Monkeys hoot. The smell of the forest is thick and fresh. During one stretch on a boat, pink dolphins swam near us. These waters also held piranhas (sounds like per-RON-ahs). For meals, we sharpened tree branches, then speared and grilled fish.

Then we'd toss the bones in the water for the piranhas to devour. Some people have the wrong idea about piranhas. These fish have teeth, but they aren't aggressive. I found that out for sure after I dropped my only pair of sunglasses in the water one day. Our guides and I jumped in the water to look for them. Luckily, the piranhas were very polite. They didn't even nibble!

Large chunks of ice can be seen in the glacier-fed lake.

Chapter 2

CHILLY IN CHILE

The glacier-fed lake stretched out in front of us. I held my breath and jumped in. The frigid water zapped my body like a shock of electricity. I felt a rush of energy and swam as fast as I could. It wouldn't be long before my body temperature dipped dangerously low.

Today was not a good day for a swim. It was cold, and we had been out of food for more than a day. I was swimming because I had no choice. The day hadn't started out badly. We were in Chile (sounds like CHEEL-ay). We had a map that showed clear trails on both sides of a nearby lake called Lago Invernada (sounds like LAY-go een-vare-NATH-uh).

Having a map was a big deal. We had started our Andes trek with a map of South America like one you might find on a wall in a classroom. It had names of towns and major rivers, but nothing else. I looked for detailed terrain maps in every town. If I did find one, it was often old and outdated. Often these maps didn't reflect important changes like recent volcanic eruptions, floods, or earthquakes that would change the landscape.

Without the benefit of good maps, we

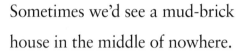

mostly relied on the kindness of the Andean people. We found useful guides in sheepherders. Sometimes we'd see a mud-brick house in the middle of nowhere.

The people we met were usually friendly. They'd often share soup, meat, or fresh carrots with us. When it came to giving directions, they'd show us the way with a friendly flick of the wrist. It sure wasn't a modern navigation system, but it worked.

Today, hunger had us walking faster than usual. If we could get to the other side of the lake, we could resupply. We imagined resting there and eating until we were full.

It wasn't long before we could see the lake. But the excitement about our long-overdue meal quickly turned into dread. The trails were not there.

The area had been flooded. All that remained were sheer cliffs surrounding the water. Our map had failed us. A half mile (0.8 km) of icy water in the flooded lake now separated us from that meal.

As the shock and disappointment began to wear off, we realized we had to move forward somehow. To us, spending another hungry night on the wrong side of the lake was not an option. We tried to think through our other options. Climbing the rocks seemed like the best choice. Swimming would be a dangerous last resort.

Generosity in the Andes

The incredible generosity of the Andean people inspired me. Villagers might never have seen an outsider before, but they always shared their food and their homes. One night in Bolivia, we met a man on a trail. He insisted we meet his family. We ate soup late into the night in his mud-brick home. We shared stories and slept on a warm sheepskin. The next day, as we walked through beautiful farmland, the people saw us off with warm wishes.

So we set out to climb. The cliff walls that surrounded the lake were very steep. Before long, we realized we were trapped. There was nothing to grab onto and nowhere to go. Reluctantly, we climbed back down.

That left only one option: Swim. Swimming was dangerous, though. We risked hypothermia (sounds like hi-poe-THUR-mee-uh). Or drowning.

The sun was sinking fast. If we were going to try this, we needed to move while there was still daylight. We waterproofed our packs as best we could and dove into the water.

Did You Know?

Normal body temperature is around 98.6°F (37°C). Hypothermia occurs as your body temperature passes below 95°F (35°C). It can be a life-threatening condition.

We quickly learned that our bodies couldn't handle the icy water. After about 10 minutes of swimming, we had to haul ourselves out of the water and take refuge on a rocky ledge. There, we dripped and shivered and moved around to keep warm.

I tried to think of what to do next. I wanted to warm up so we could swim more. But it was a race against the sun, and we had lost. We spent a long, uncomfortable night shivering in our sleeping bags on that rock. We were both scared. We couldn't tell how far we'd have to swim in the morning to get to the other side. At least we'd have the sun.

In the morning, we slept as late as we could to give the sun time to warm things up. We waterproofed all of our clothes and sleeping bags again. We were ready to go, but the weather was not.

A fierce wind had kicked up. For 45 minutes, we sat and waited for it to die down. Unbelievably, the conditions were colder and scarier than the day before.

While we waited, we tried to come up with a solution. We looked for other routes. Could we go up? Maybe around? Back over the rocks? No. In the end, there was nothing but the bitter-cold water.

When we finally jumped in again, the water seemed to cut into my body like a knife. I wasn't sure how we could survive this.

Because we couldn't endure the water for long, we had to always be on the lookout for rocks to swim to. We'd heave ourselves onto the rocks like seals. We'd try to dry off a little in the sun and warm ourselves with tea that we'd make with our stove. The agony of the cold and wet almost made us forget we hadn't eaten in two days.

Thirty-six hours after our first plunge the night before, we reached the other side of the lake. It was early evening. We were shivering and numb. My face was chapped from the wind and wet and cold.

As the sun set, we headed toward the village. I'm not sure I've ever been hungrier. I looked over my shoulder at the far shore of the lake where we started. I felt lucky to have survived.

Did You Know?

Being tired and dehydrated can increase your risk of hypothermia.

Gregg continues his hike through the Atacama Desert.

Chapter 3

BEAUTIFUL PUZZLE

A sound like stampeding horses woke me up in the night. I had my sleeping bag set up under a juniper (sounds like JOO-nuh-pur) tree in the desert. We had passed through a tiny town at the northern end of the Atacama (sounds like ah-ta-COMM-ah) Desert in northern Chile. I sat up and saw something large dart past me.

I put on my sandals and slowly got up. As my eyes adjusted to the dark, I saw a pair of large, green eyes about 20 feet (6 m) away. They looked in my direction. I held my breath.

This was a puma on the hunt. I knew a puma was unlikely to attack a human unless I got in its way. I backed up slowly until I felt my sleeping bag behind me. I knew the puma must be aware of me and that it could see better than I could in the dark. Suddenly, I wished I were invisible.

After a while, it moved on, and I climbed back into my sleeping bag.

But I didn't sleep much that night. In the morning, I found footprints of the large cat. We had seen puma tracks and even the occasional hair ball on desert trails, but I had never been so close to one of these amazing predators. I was in awe of its stealth and power.

That day, as we faced the start of a 200-mile (322-km) stretch of hiking, I thought about how it might feel to be a puma, hungry and struggling to survive in the desert. I wanted to understand the beautiful puzzle of nature and help protect it.

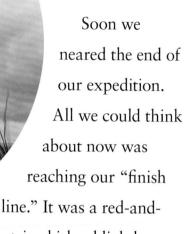

Soon we neared the end of our expedition. All we could think about now was reaching our "finish line." It was a red-and-white-striped island lighthouse in Tierra del Fuego (sounds like tee-AIR-uh del FWEY-goh). So far, we had hiked more than 7,800 miles (12,552 km). But the Andes weren't going to let us go easily.

In the final weeks, days of hiking through peat bogs slowed our progress. During the day, relentless, deep mud sucked at our shoes and exhausted our muscles. At night, we tried to pitch our tent in the driest spot we could find. But we'd only get about half an hour of sleep before the tent filled up with water.

Night after night, we'd lie there shivering, wishing for sleep. Then, we'd get up, gather all of our wet, heavy gear, and walk in the dark just to get warm.

Once we made it to the island of Tierra del Fuego, we knew we were close. We crested ridge after ridge, hoping to see that lighthouse. It seemed like it was never going to happen. Then I heard Deia shriek. We had made it. Our shouts of joy echoed off the rock walls behind us. We lingered over our final steps to the lighthouse. I marveled at each last piece of grass and dirt. We were at the end of the continent.

It's strange, but I didn't feel the relief I expected. It was exciting to get to the end, but I hated to leave the beauty of the Andes and the kindness of the people who live there.

I would go home with the eyes of an explorer, at least, ready to take on the next challenge. I started thinking again about how it only takes three seconds of courage to follow your dream.

Now I knew my dream was to be of service to animals. I wanted to make choices that would benefit them. Becoming a biologist was a first step for me. The following year, I earned a degree in ecology (sounds like ee-KAH-luh-jee) from Montana State University. Within a year of returning from the Andes, I was working as a field biologist, tracking owls in the forests of California and studying

endangered sturgeon
(sounds like STUR-juhn)
fish. Not long after that,
I started a new kind of
journey, founding the nonprofit
organization Adventure Scientists.

Since then, I have led Adventure Science
expeditions and other scientific missions
in Botswana, Uganda, and Mongolia, as
well as in the Mojave (sounds like moh-
HAH-vee) Desert, Alaska, and Hawaii in
the United States.

Hunger, cold, and pain have been a
part of every one of my expeditions. But
each one has also been an opportunity
for me to persevere and use my creativity.
I don't know what my next adventure
will be. I only know that I will be ready.

Kids Can Make a Difference

You don't have to be a biologist to make a positive impact on the world. All it takes to help save the environment is the courage to do something that helps. There are many things you can do. You can be a conservationist at home. Pick up litter in your neighborhood or at school. Turn off the water while brushing your teeth. Keep lights turned off, and eat local food. It all adds up to reduce the pressure on our planet's natural resources.

THE END

DON'T MISS!

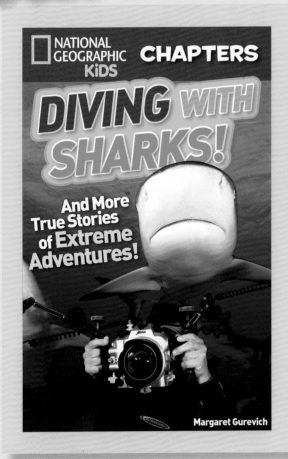

NATIONAL GEOGRAPHIC KiDS **CHAPTERS**

DIVING WITH SHARKS!

And More True Stories of Extreme Adventures!

Margaret Gurevich

Turn the page for a sneak preview . . .

DAVID DOUBILET AND JENNIFER HAYES: DIVING WITH SHARKS!

Photographer David Doubilet comes face-to-face with some Caribbean reef sharks.

A tiger shark feeds on a dead sperm whale.

Chapter 1

FACE-TO-FACE

The radio on the boat crackled to life. David Doubilet and his wife and diving partner, Jennifer Hayes, listened closely. A dead sperm whale had been sighted off the reef of Cairns in Australia. This was rare. There had not been a sperm whale carcass sighting in 30 years. Ten large tiger sharks were feeding on the whale. David knew they had to photograph it.

It's unusual to see sharks feeding in the wild. Sometimes sharks are hand-fed during tours so tourists can dive and see them. David and Jennifer knew that this natural feeding would be a special opportunity.

They set the boat's coordinates (sounds like co-ORE-din-its) to where the whale had been spotted, and sped along the water as fast as they could. Yet when they arrived at their destination, there was no whale to be seen. The wind and tide had moved it, but where?

David and Jennifer scanned the water. Finally, they saw a large mass floating on the ocean's surface. They breathed a sigh of relief. It was the whale.

The whale's white flesh was oozing whale oil. The strong smell filled the air.

And eight large tiger sharks circled the carcass. It was time for David and Jennifer to get a closer look.

David and Jennifer slipped into the water. From there, they had a much better view. The sharks' teeth ripped into the whale's body, tearing it to shreds. David and Jennifer raised their cameras and began taking pictures.

They knew that as long as they kept their distance from the sharks, they'd be safe. After all, the sharks were busy eating the whale. But they had taken some precautions (sounds like pree-COSH-ens), just in case. Both were wearing full diving gear. "We always wear full wet suits, including gloves that cover our hands," said Jennifer. "Our bare hands look a lot like dead fish and may be tempting to a shark used to seeing dead fish as food." They also had their cameras. In some ways, those big cameras helped the team feel safer. It was like having an extra layer of protection between them and the sharks.

So, David and Jennifer focused on shooting pictures. The sharks focused on their meal. In fact, the sharks didn't seem to notice David and Jennifer at all.

But as they kept taking pictures, David and Jennifer didn't realize they were getting closer and closer to the tiger sharks and their carcass. The sharks noticed, though. Suddenly, the mood changed.

The sharks were interested in the two humans bobbing in the water.

David and Jennifer looked around. They had somehow drifted too close to the whale. Now, the sharks saw them as a threat. Finding food in the ocean can be hard, and sharks will protect their meal. David and Jennifer weren't safe anymore.

The sharks began to circle. They swam close enough to bump into David and Jennifer. That's when the photographers thought about their "extra layer of protection." They held their cameras in front of them to block the sharks.

Suddenly, one of the sharks lunged forward. It bit at one of the large, round strobe lights attached to the cameras. Other sharks did the same.

Working Together

David and Jennifer are married, and they work together, too! On land, they have different jobs. David prepares their camera gear and lights. Jennifer researches their subjects and talks with experts. Underwater, they work as a team. To make sure they understand each other underwater, they use hand signals. Or they write using a dive slate and pencil. In dangerous situations, David and Jennifer wear face masks with voice gear so they can talk to each other—that's the clearest form of communication.

Strobes are normally used to light up dark areas. But now they were being used as shark shields!

David and Jennifer needed a way to fend off the sharks until they could swim to safety. They changed their position in the water and put their backs against each other. This way they could see all around them. They could see where the sharks were. That would keep them safe.

They began to swim slowly away from the sharks and toward their boat. The key was to keep their movements small. If they moved too quickly, the sharks would react ...

INDEX

Boldface indicates illustrations.

MORE INFORMATION

Adventure Scientists (adventurescience.org) is a nonprofit organization based in Bozeman, Montana, U.S.A. The organization matches extreme outdoor athletes (like hikers, paddlers, and skiers) with information-hungry scientists who need data samples from hard-to-reach places all over the world.

Since its founding in 2011, the nonprofit has sent thousands of specialized adventurers on missions to collect data from remote and challenging locations for their conservation partners. These partnerships have led to the discovery of more than two dozen new species, provided key information to guide climate change decision-making, and helped protect threatened wildlife habitat around the world.

CREDITS

For my family, who has stood by me through all the challenges, both good and bad. And my wife, Whitney, who helps me navigate the many different journeys of life. —GT

ACKNOWLEDGMENTS

I would like to thank Mrs. Miller, who thought I was worth her extra time, my grandma Ann for long walks in the metro parks, the National Geographic Society for its relentless support, and our team at Adventure Scientists, who work tirelessly to make the world a better place. I'd also like to thank Kitson Jazynka and Shelby Alinsky for their help in producing and writing this book. And a special thank-you to my friends and family, who embrace my crazy. —GT

AUTHOR'S NOTE

The danger of my expeditions has always been an exciting aspect for me. But, more important, the adventure and the opportunity to connect with nature is what draws me back into the wilderness time and again. I have learned to plan carefully for the dangers I may face—it's important to stay safe when you're so far from help. And I have learned that when the unexpected happens, it's important to stay calm. When you plan ahead, it leaves you more time to explore, learn, and enjoy your adventure!